My First Toddler Coloring Book
numbers shapes counting Coloring

Baby Activity Book for Kids Age 1-3, Boys or Girls
Easy Learning of First Easy Words about Shapes and Numbers

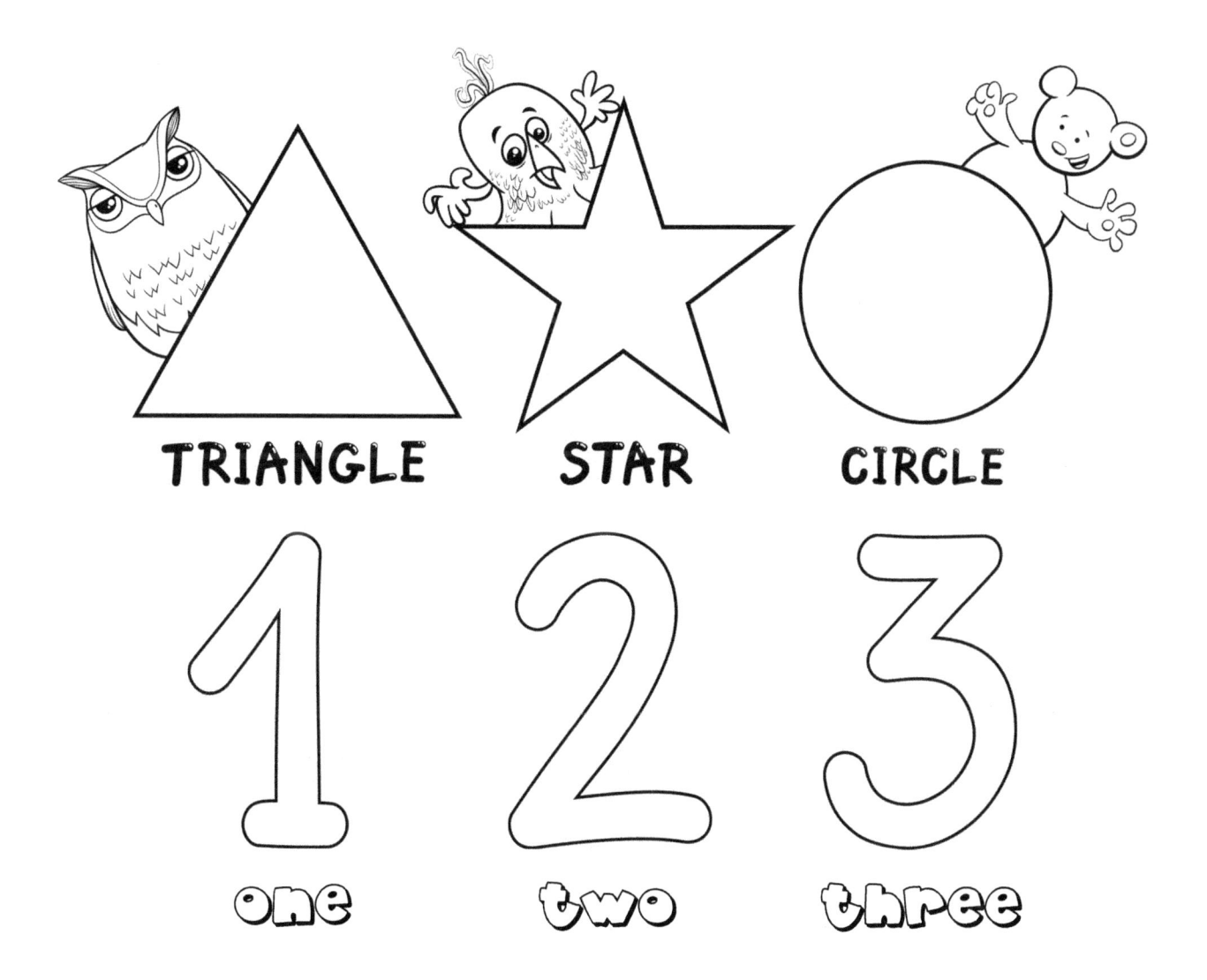

TRIANGLE   STAR   CIRCLE

1   2   3

one   two   three

Copyright 2018

All rights reserved. No part of this publication may be reproduced, stored in a retrieval system, or transmitted in any form or by any means, electronic, mechanical, photocopying, recording or otherwise, without the prior written permission of the publisher.

Printed by CreateSpace, An Amazon.com Company
A Publication by Coloring Books For Toddlers

CIRCLE

TRIANGLE

SQUARE

ELLIPSE

RECTANGLE

PENTAGON

DIAMOND

CRESCENT

STAR

CROSS

zero

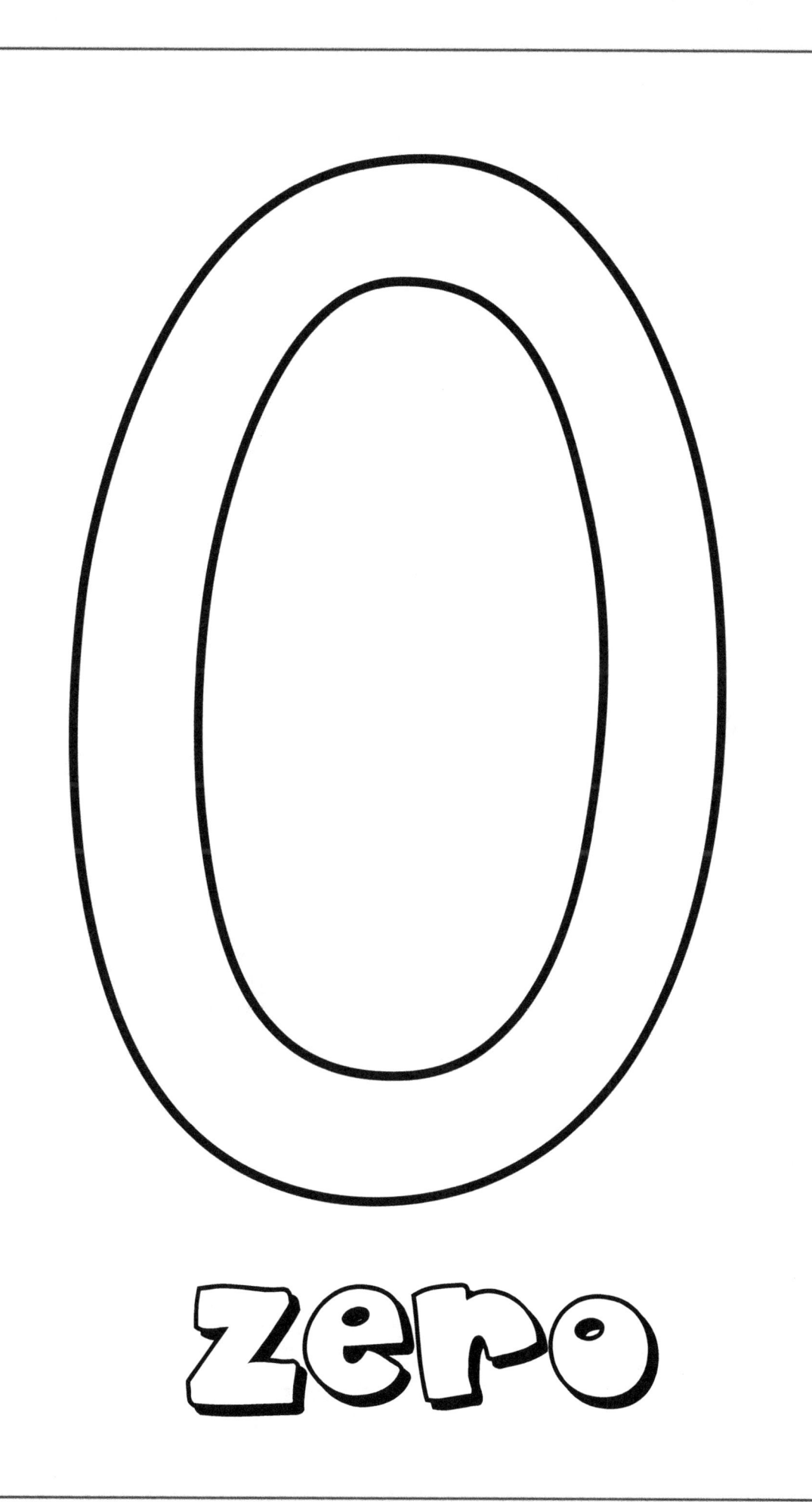

1

one

2
two

3

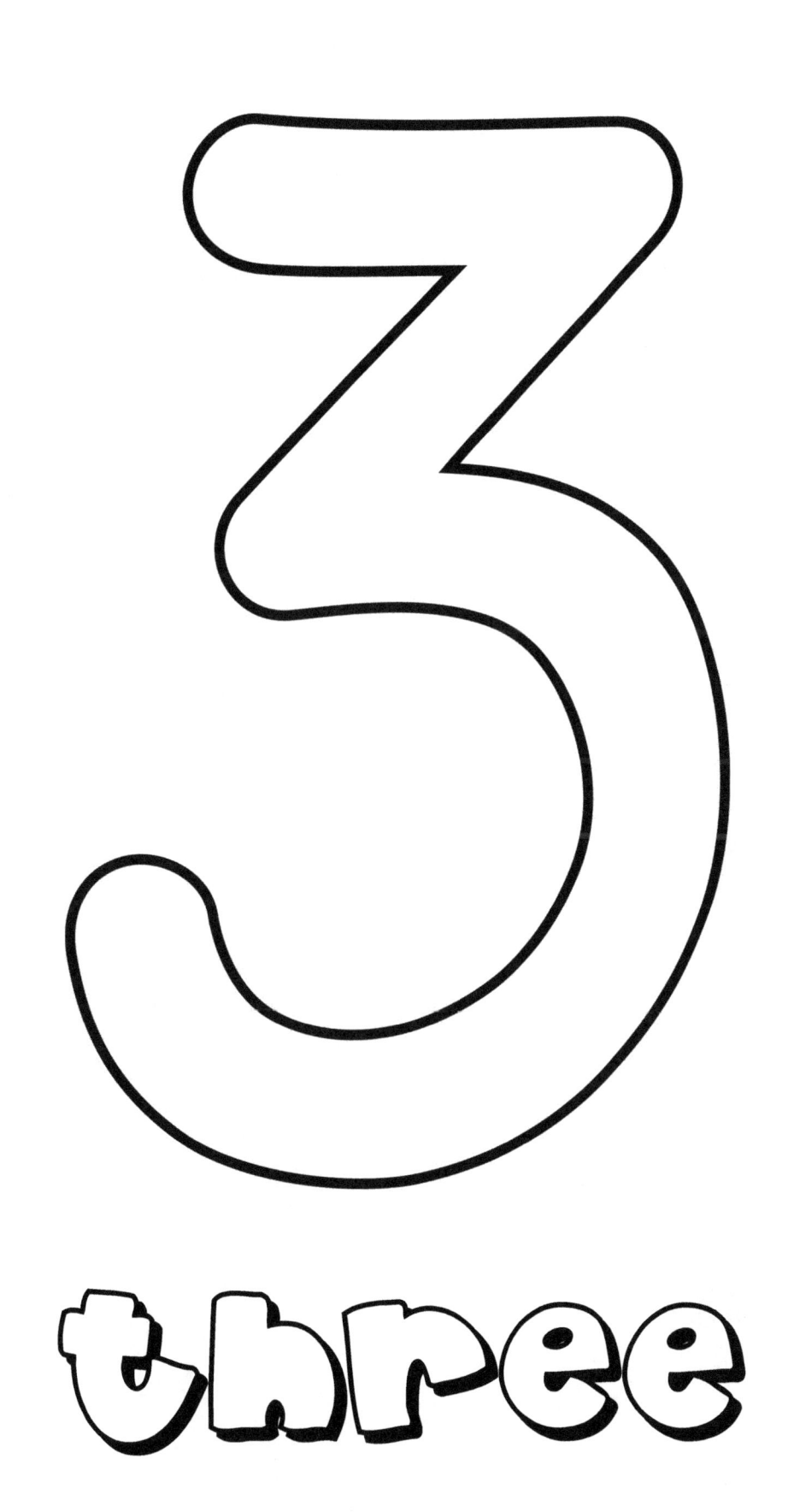

three

4

four

5

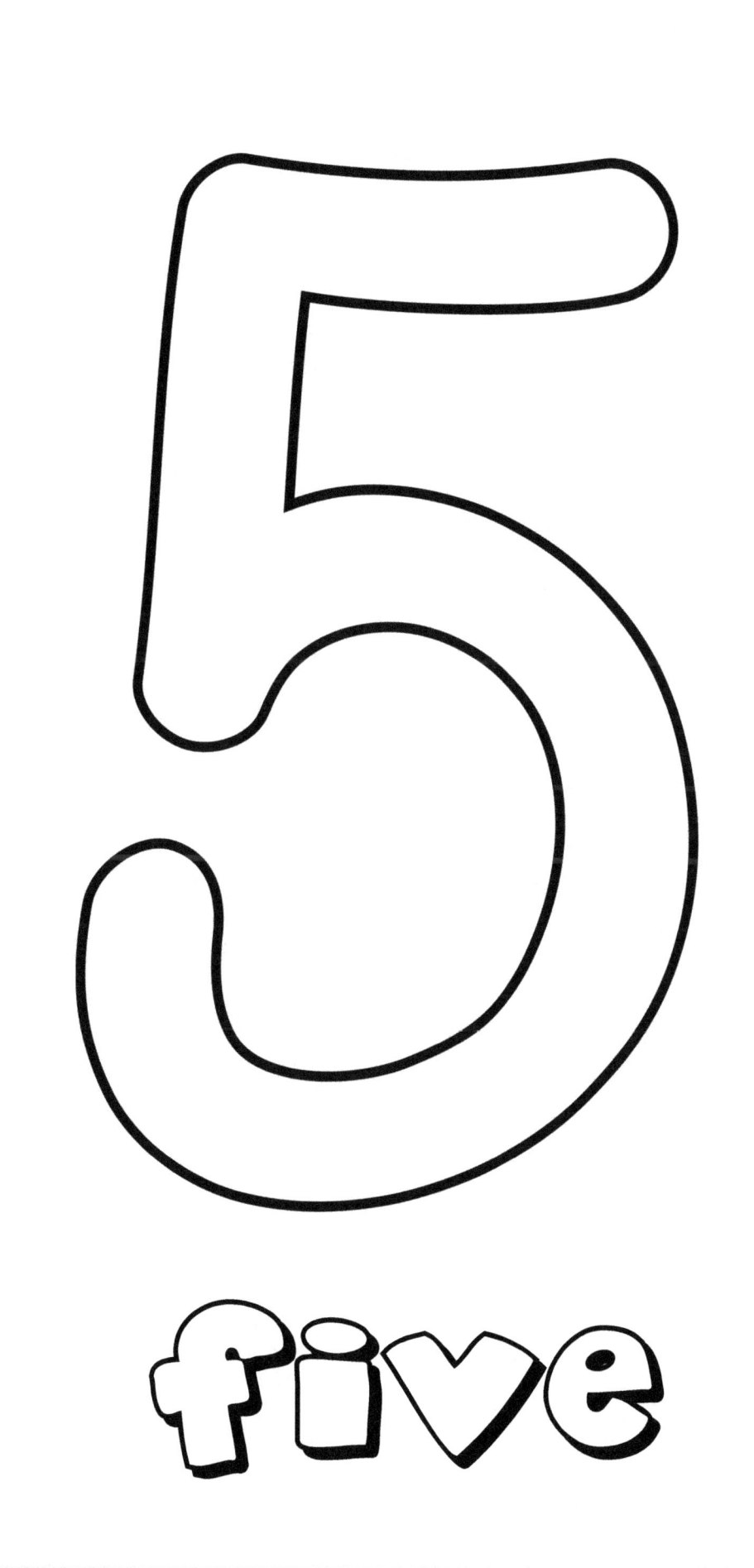

five

6

six

7

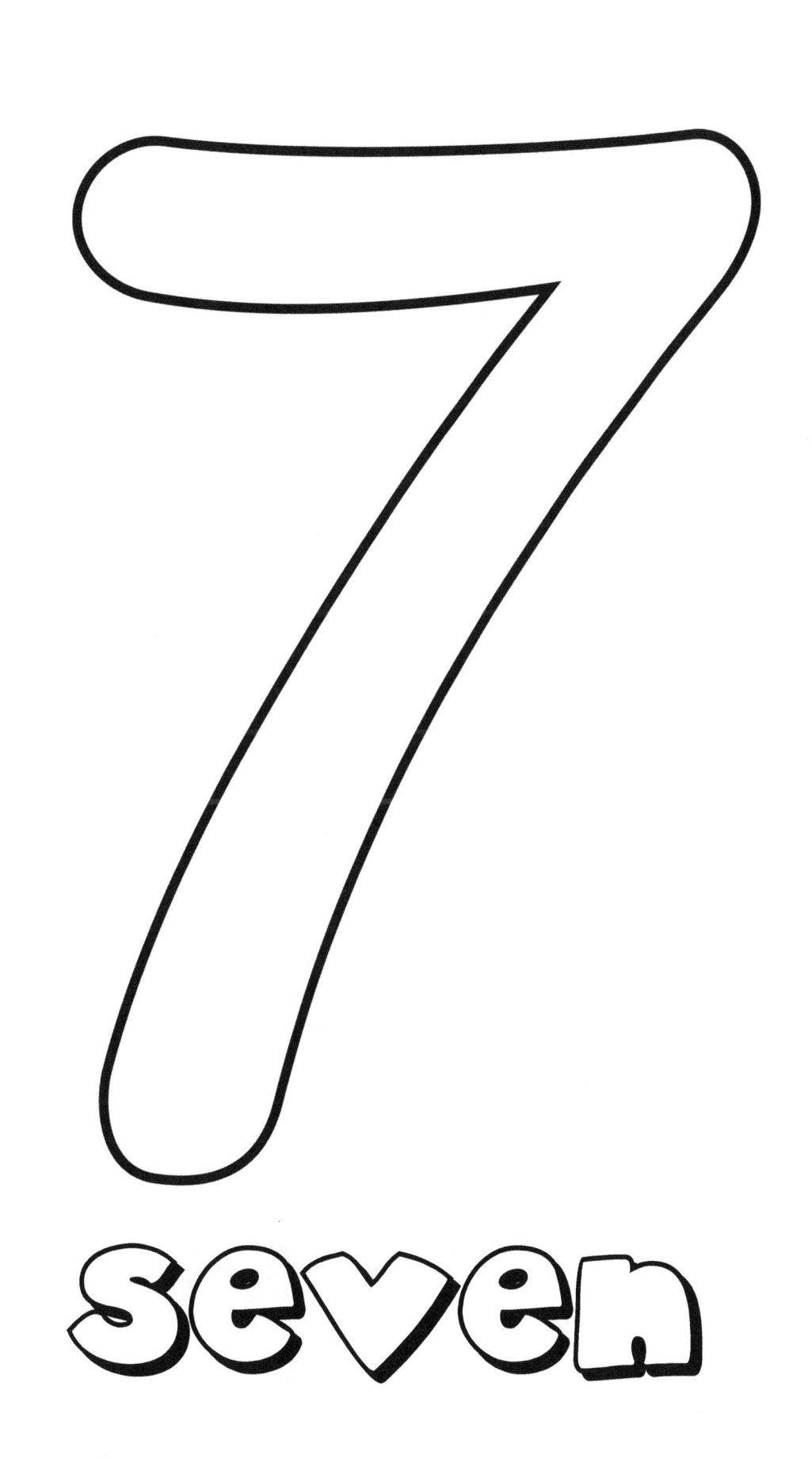

seven

8

eight

9

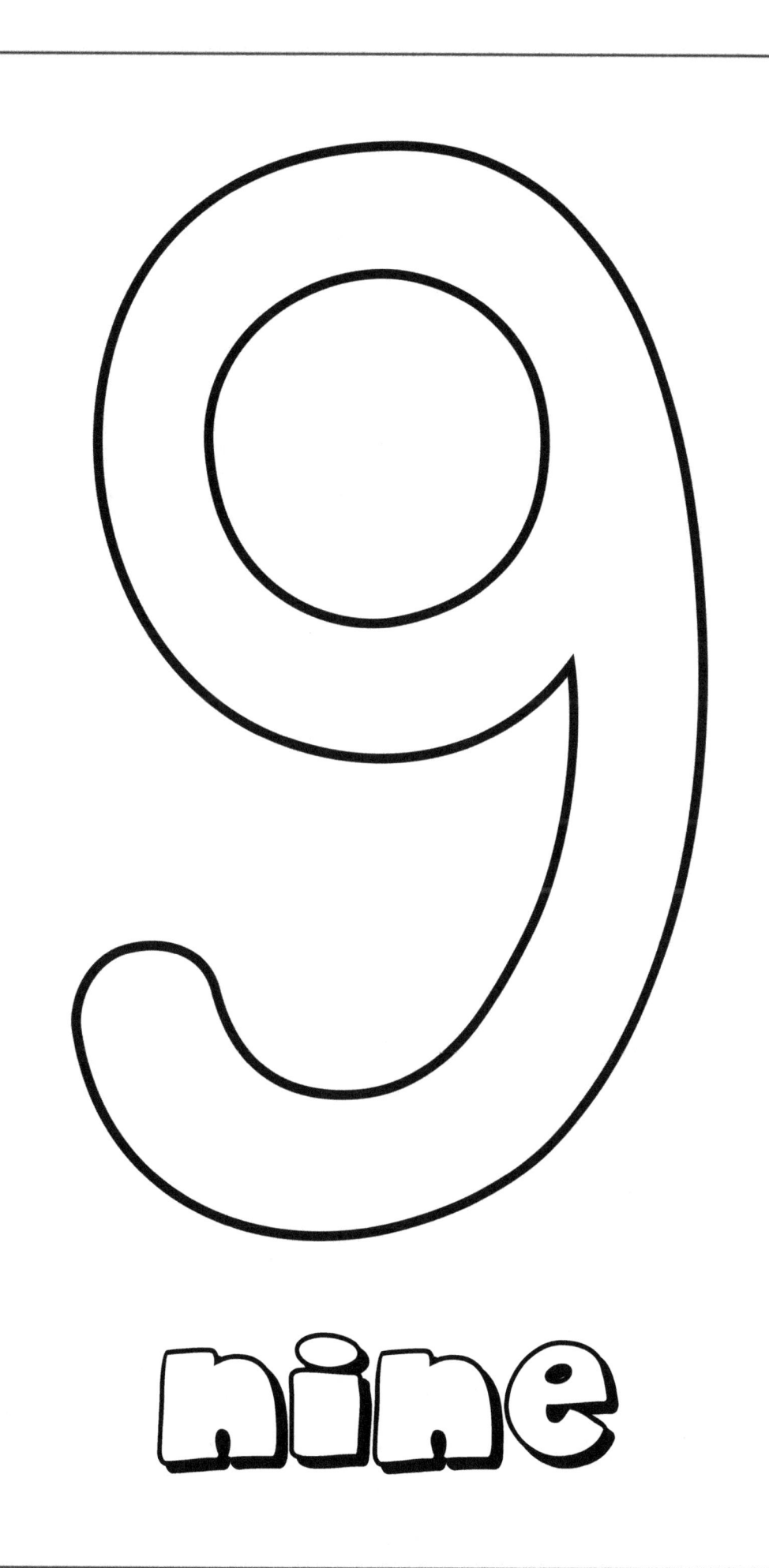

nine

10
ten

one

1

2

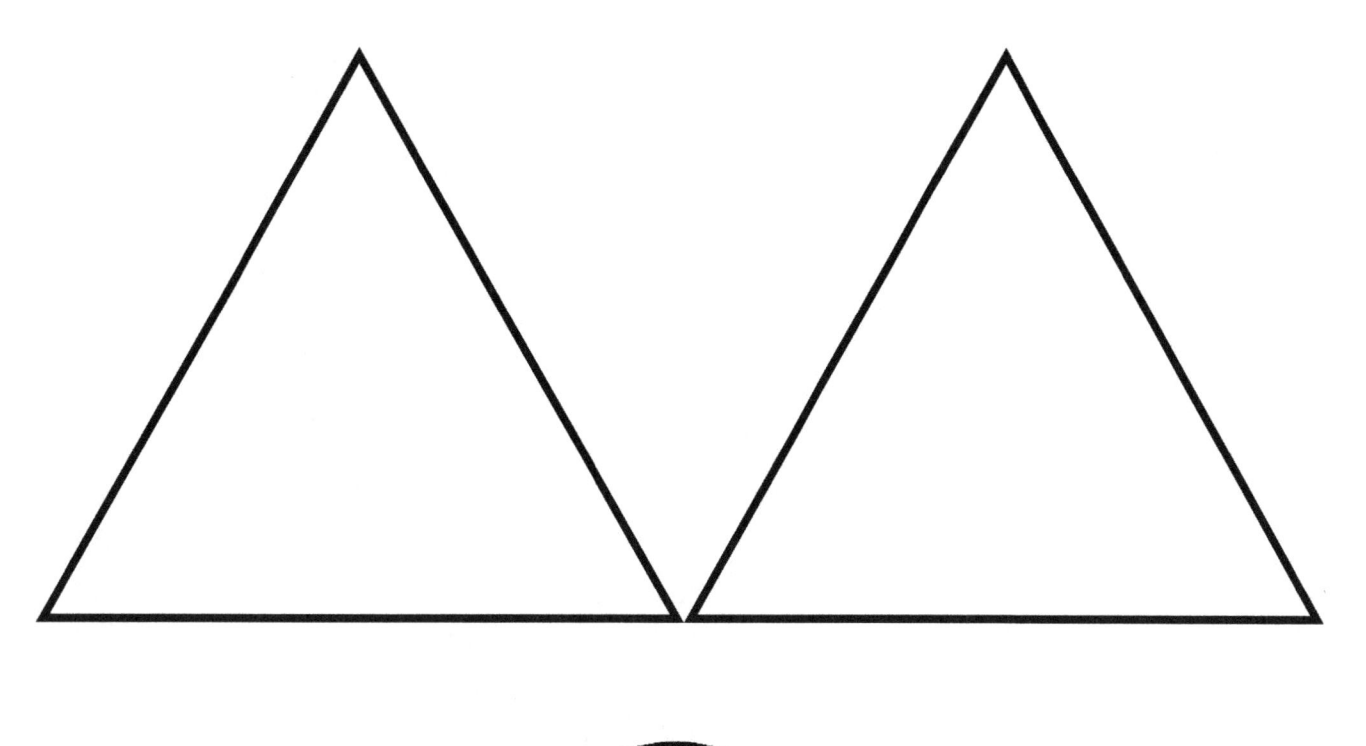

two

3

three

four 4

5

five

six 6

7

seven

8

eight

nine 9

10 ten

CPSIA information can be obtained
at www.ICGtesting.com
Printed in the USA
BVHW011947170220
572595BV00009B/376